Passive cash flow
25 Passive Income Ideas To Increase Your Earnings in 2024.

Wendy H. Williams

Table of Contents

Part one

- Passive income: what is it?

Regular profits from a source other than an employer or contractor are considered passive income. According to the Internal Revenue Service (IRS), there are two ways to earn passive income: renting out real estate or taking part in a business but not actively running it, such as receiving stock dividends or book royalties. Although that is accurate in law, passive income can arrive in other forms.

According to financial advisor and former hedge fund manager Todd Tresidder, "Many people think that passive income is about getting something for nothing." It has an appeal to "get rich quick." But in the end, work is still required. You simply provide the labor up ahead.

In reality, you might have to put in a lot of work upfront, but earning passive money frequently requires additional work in the process. To continue receiving passive income, you might need to maintain your rental property or keep your product updated.

However, if you stick with the plan, it can be a terrific method to make money and you'll end up with some extra financial security.

Locating a knowledgeable financial advisor to help you make the most significant financial decisions of your life is simple.
It's not passive income
Your position. In general, revenue from anything you've been tangibly involved in—like your salary from a job—is not considered passive income.
an additional employment. Acquiring a second job won't make it count as a passive income source because you'll still have to put in the work and be compensated for it. The goal of passive income is to generate a steady flow of money without requiring you to put in a lot of labor.

assets that don't generate revenue. If your assets are paying dividends or interest, investing might be a terrific strategy to create passive income. Although they could be fascinating, non-dividend-paying stocks and other assets like cryptocurrencies won't provide you with passive income.

- Establish a course

Making an audio or video course and then sitting back while money comes in from sales is a well-liked method for generating passive income. Sites like Udemy, SkillShare, and Coursera are platforms for the distribution and sale of courses.

An alternative is to think about a "freemium model," which involves providing free content to attract readers and charging for more in-depth information or for those who are interested in learning more. This approach can be used, for instance, by language instructors and investment selection advisors. The complimentary material showcases your proficiency and can draw in individuals who want to advance.

Possibility: Since you can quickly make money after the initial time investment, taking a course can be a great way to generate revenue.

Risk: "Creating the product requires a tremendous amount of work," according to Tresidder. And it needs to be excellent to generate good money. There isn't any space for rubbish outside.

If you want to succeed, you need to create a solid platform, promote your goods, and make plans for other products.

"Unless you get really lucky, one product does not make a business."To increase sales of an already-existing product, additional superior products need to be made.

You can create a reliable source of revenue once you have
mastered the company model.

  • Compose an electronic book.
Writing an e-book can be a great way to benefit from the cheap cost of publication and even use Amazon's global distribution to get your book in front of millions of prospective readers. Because they are based on your knowledge, e-books can be quite short—perhaps 30 to 50 pages—and inexpensive to produce.

You'll need to be an authority on a particular subject, yet it may be specialized and call for knowledge or skills that are uncommon but that many readers require. Using an online platform, you can rapidly design the book and even test-market several titles and price points.

However, much as when creating a course, the majority of the benefit arises from including additional e-books in the mix and attracting more readers to your material.

Possibility: An e-book can serve as a vehicle for directing readers to your other products, such as audio or video courses, other e-books, a website, or possibly more expensive seminars, in addition to providing them with useful information.

Risk: To gain a following, your e-book needs to be good. It also helps if you have a marketing strategy in place, such as an existing website, a promotion on other websites that are relevant to it, media appearances, podcast appearances, or something else. Thus, especially in the beginning, you can work extremely hard and receive very little in return for your efforts.

Even while an e-book is great, it will be beneficial if you write more and even create a business around it, or even simply make the book a component that supports your other offerings. Therefore, the biggest risk you face is generally squandering time for lit tle return.

Chapter three

Rental revenue

One efficient method of generating passive income is through rental property investments. But people frequently underestimate how much work is involved.

You can lose more money than you invested if you don't take the time to figure out how to make it lucrative.

Opportunity: There are three things you need to decide to generate passive income from rental properties:

How much of an investment return you're looking for

The overall expenses and charges for the property

Financial concerns associated with property ownership

For instance, to achieve your target of $10,000 annually in rental cash flow, you would need to charge $3,133 in rent each month in addition to the $2,000 monthly mortgage, $300 for taxes, and other costs associated with the property.

Risk: There are a few things to think about: Does your property have a market? What happens if the renter damages the property or makes late payments? If you can't find a tenant for your property, what then? Any of these elements could significantly reduce your passive income.

Economic downturns can also present difficulties. You might still have a mortgage to pay, but your tenants might all of a sudden be unable to make their rent payments. Or, if revenues fall, you might not be able to rent out the house for as much as you could previously. Additionally, rent may not be enough to meet your expenses because property prices climbed swiftly, partly due to comparatively cheap mortgage rates. To safeguard yourself, you should consider these dangers and make backup measures.

- Affiliate advertising

By putting a link to a third party's goods on their website or social media account, bloggers, social media "influencers," and website owners can promote the product through affiliate marketing. Although eBay, Awin, and ShareASale are among the bigger brands in the affiliate space, Amazon is arguably the most well-known partner. Furthermore, TikTok and Instagram have developed into significant channels for anyone trying to market their goods and build a following.

You might also think about building an email list to promote your blog or point them in the direction of other goods and services they might find useful.

Possibility: The website owner receives a commission if a visitor clicks on the link and purchases something from the third-party affiliate. It may take a considerable amount of visitors to your website to make a substantial profit, as the commission could vary from 3 to 7 percent. However, you might be able to make a significant amount of money if you can expand your fan base or focus on a more lucrative area (such as software, financial services, or fitness).

Because you can theoretically make money by just posting a link to your website or social media account, affiliate marketing is regarded as passive. If you can't get visitors to visit your website, click on the link, and make a purchase, you won't get paid at all.

Risk: Creating content and increasing traffic will take time if you're just getting started.

Building a following can take a long time, and finding the ideal formula to draw in that audience is a process that may take some time in and of itself. Even worse, your following can abandon you for the next big influencer, fad, or social media site after you've expended all that effort.

• Turn around retail merchandise
Profit from internet marketplaces like eBay and Amazon by listing items that you discover elsewhere for significantly less money. In addition to profiting from the discrepancy between your purchase and sale prices, you might be able to cultivate a following of people who watch your transactions.

Possibility: You can profit from pricing discrepancies between what you can find and what the typical customer would be able to find. If you know someone who can assist you get reduced goods that not many people can find, this might work very effectively.

Alternatively, you can discover worthwhile items that people have just missed.

Risk: Although internet sales can occur at any time, which helps to make this technique passive, you'll need to work hard to locate a dependable supplier of goods. Additionally, you'll need a steady stream of income because you'll need to invest in each of your products until they sell. To ensure that you are not purchasing at an excessive price, you will need to have a thorough understanding of the market. If not, you can find yourself with things that nobody wants or that you have to significantly lower to sell.

Part two

- Make money online by selling photos

Although it might not seem like the best idea to start a passive business selling photographs online, you could be able to increase your efforts if you can sell the same images often. You may collaborate with a company like Getty Images, Shutterstock, or Alamy to do that.

You must first obtain platform approval before you may license your images for use by anyone who downloads them. Every time someone uses your photo on the platform, you are paid by it.

You'll need to identify the areas where demand is highest and find images that speak to a particular demographic or depict a particular scene. Images may depict landscapes, creative settings, models, or real-life events that could be featured in the media.

Possibility of scaling up: If you can supply images that will be in demand, scaling up your efforts is one of the benefits of selling or licensing your photos through a platform. This implies that you might be able to sell the same picture hundreds, thousands, or even more times.

Risk: It's possible to upload hundreds of images to a website like Getty Images and have none of them lead to significant sales. You need to keep posting photographs while you try to find the proverbial "needle in the haystack" because only a handful of them might generate all of your income.

Going out and taking pictures, processing them, and staying up to date with the events that could eventually drive your revenue could take a lot of work. Additionally, it could be difficult to stay motivated: although it's unlikely, every picture you take could be your lott
every ticket.

- Invest in real estate crowdsourcing

Using a crowdfunding platform to purchase real estate is an additional choice if you're interested in investing in real estate but don't want to handle most of the administrative work, maintenance, tenant relations, and other tasks. Once the real estate has been selected by a skilled investing team, you can determine how much you are comfortable investing in it.

The real estate platform will charge you an annual management fee, and the minimum investment amounts you can make could be anywhere from ten dollars to tens of thousands of dollars.

Possibility: You have access to private real estate transactions that have been prescreened by experienced investors and may prove to be appealing. To get a sense of the kind of returns you might anticipate and over what duration, you can review the returns on the platforms. Investing in real estate can also diversify your holdings and improve return consistency.

While some platforms invest in debt, others in equity (stock). In general, debt offers lower returns for less risk, whereas stocks offer higher returns for more risk. A particular amount of assets or an accredited investor status are prerequisites for various platforms. Several well-known platforms are DiversyFund, Yieldstreet, and Fundrise.

Risk: With many crowdfunding platforms, you are responsible for making your investments. Hence, even if past performance may seem favorable, it cannot guarantee future results. Additionally, you'll need to use your judgment while deciding what to buy. This implies that you will have to study the prospectus and weigh the advantages and disadvantages of each transaction you are considering.

In addition, real estate is often funded with large levels of debt financing, making it more sensitive to any economic downturn. Particularly in an emergency, you should know how long your money will be locked up in the investment and when you can retrieve it.

- Mutual-to-peer financing

Peer-to-peer, or P2P, loans are personal loans made between a borrower and yourself that are handled by an intermediary like Prosper. Upstart and LendingClub are two more participants.

Possibility: The interest payments made on the loans provide you with income as a lender. However, in the event of a default, you might receive nothing because the loan is unsecured.

Two actions are necessary to reduce that risk:

Spread out your smaller investments among several loans to diversify your lending portfolio. The minimum loan investment at Prosper.com is $25.

Examine past information on the potential borrowers to make well-informed decisions.

Risk: P2P lending is not completely passive; you will need to thoroughly screen potential borrowers as it takes some time to become proficient in its criteria. Given that you are investing in several loans, you need to be particularly aware of the payments that you get. If you wish to increase your income, you should reinvest whatever interest you earn.

High-yielding personal loans may also be more likely to default during economic recessions, meaning that as things go worse, they may default at rates higher than i
n the past.

- Dividend stocks

Shareholders in companies with dividend-yielding stocks receive a payment at regular intervals from the company. Companies pay cash dividends every quarter out of their profits, and all you need to do is own the stock. Dividends are paid per share of stock, so the more shares you own, the higher your payout. Opportunity: Since the income from the stocks isn't related to any activity other than the initial financial investment, owning dividend-yielding stocks can be one of the most passive forms of making money. The money will simply be deposited in your brokerage account. Risk: The tricky part is choosing the right stocks. For example, companies issuing a very high dividend may not be able to sustain it. Too many novices jump into the market without thoroughly investigating the company issuing the stock. "You've got to investigate each company's website and be comfortable with their financial statements "You should spend two to three weeks investigating each company." That said, there are ways to invest in dividend-yielding stocks without spending a huge amount of time evaluating companies. Going with exchange-traded funds, or ETFs. ETFs are investment funds that hold assets such as stocks, commodities, and bonds, but they trade like stocks. ETFs also diversify your holdings, so if one company cuts its payout, it doesn't affect the ETF's price or dividend too much. Here are some of the best ETFs to choose from. "ETFs are an ideal choice for novices because they are easy to understand, highly liquid, inexpensive, and have far better potential returns because of far lower costs than mutual funds," Graves says. Another key risk is that stocks or ETFs can move down significantly in short periods, especially during times of uncertainty, as in 2020 when the coronavirus crisis shocked financial markets. Economic stress can also cause some companies to cut their dividends entirely, while diversified funds may feel less of a pinch.

- Develop an application.

Making an app might be a means to put in the initial time commitment and then get paid later on. Your app may be a game or a tool to assist consumers with difficult tasks on their mobile devices. Users download your program after it's made public, which allows you to make money.

Possibility: If you can create an app that appeals to your target user base, there are a lot of opportunities. You must think about the best way to make money off of your software. For instance, you may charge customers a small fee to download the app or you may display in-app advertisements.

You will probably need to add little additions to your app to keep it current and well-liked if it becomes more popular or if you get feedback.

Risk: Using your time inefficiently is arguably the largest risk here. You have minimal financial risk if you invest little to no money in the project (or money that you would have spent on hardware, for example). It's a competitive business, though, so apps that succeed must provide users with an engaging experience or value.

Additionally, you should confirm that should your app gather any data, it complies with local, national, and international privacy regulations. Additionally, the popularity of apps might fade quickly, so you might not have as much income flow as you had antiicpated.

Part three

- Lease a parking place.

Is there a parking spot you have available that you might utilize for someone else? That space could be exchanged for some cash. If you have a bigger space that could accommodate numerous automobiles or be used for other events or places, it might be an even better setup.

Possibility: Your parking space may be worth actual money in extremely popular locations or at popular times (like during a concert or sporting event). For instance, you may have a money-maker on your hands if you reside close to a place where parking is few but commuting traffic is high. If you rent to someone who uses the space every day as opposed to just for special occasions, you might have the best chance of making money.

Risk: While there may not be much danger associated with this notion, you should

nevertheless make sure that renting out a parking space does not violate any rules set forth by your place of residence or another organization. It's usually a good idea to include a responsibility disclaimer in the terms of parking in your p
lace.

- REITs

A real estate investment trust, or REIT for short, is a fancy term for a business that owns and operates real estate. Due to a unique legal arrangement, REITs can transmit the majority of their revenue to shareholders and pay little to no corporate income tax.

Possibility: REITs can be bought on the stock market in the same manner as dividend stocks or other companies. You will receive the dividend that the REIT pays out, and since the greatest REITs have a history of raising their payout each year, you may eventually see your dividend stream increase.

Individual REITs can be riskier to acquire than an ETF made up of several dozen REIT equities, much like dividend stocks. Investing in a fund offers instant diversification, is typically far safer than purchasing individual equities, and still yields a respectable reward.

Risk: Choosing the right REITs will require you to do a thorough and time-consuming analysis of any company you may want to purchase, much like you would with dividend stocks. Even though it's a passive pastime, if you don't know what you're doing, you could lose a lot of money. Similar to any stock, there can be significant short-term price fluctuations.

REIT distributions are also not immune to adverse economic conditions. The REIT will probably have to reduce or stop paying its dividend if it doesn't make enough money. As a result, your passive income can suffer right when you need it most.

- A ladder of bonds

A bond ladder is a group of bonds that mature over several years at various intervals. You can reduce reinvestment risk—the risk of reinvesting your money when bonds offer interest payments that are too low—by taking advantage of the staggered maturities.

Possibility: For many years, pensioners and those approaching retirement have found comfort in traditional passive investments like bond ladders. After the bond matures, you "extend the ladder," rolling over the principal into a new set of bonds, so you can relax and start collecting your interest payments. You may begin with bonds that are one, three, five, or seven years long, for instance.

Once the first bond matures in a year, you will have bonds with remaining terms of two, four, and six years. The funds from the recently matured bond can be used to purchase a new bond with one year or rolled over to a longer bond with an eight-year length.

Risk: Purchasing a bond ladder avoids one of the main hazards associated with bond investing: the possibility that you will need to purchase a new bond when interest rates are not at their best when your current bond matures.

Bonds also carry additional risks. Corporate bonds are not guaranteed by the federal government, thus in the event of a company default, you could lose your principal. Treasury bonds are. Additionally, holding multiple bonds will help you diversify your risk and remove the possibility that any one bond may negatively impact your entire portfolio. The value of your bonds may decrease if interest rates rise generally.

Bond ETFs, which offer a diversified portfolio of bonds that you can arrange into a ladder to reduce the chance of a single bond negatively affecting your returns, are popular among investors as a result of the se worries.

• Social media posts that are sponsored
Do you enjoy a sizable following on social media platforms like TikTok and Instagram? Get up-and-coming consumer brands to compensate you for promoting their goods on your feed or writing about them in your posts.

But you'll still need to consistently add engaging content to your profile. And that entails carrying on with writing social media pieces that expand your audience and interact with your followers.

Possibility: Making the most of your social media presence is a lucrative business strategy. Strong material will attract attention and clicks to your profile. You can then monetize that content by placing sponsored posts from brands that your followers would find interesting.

Danger: Beginning here may present a Catch-22 situation. To earn significant sponsored articles, you need a big audience, but until you have a meaningful audience, you are not a desirable option. As a result, you'll need to devote a lot of effort to expanding your audience without any assurance of success. It's possible to find yourself investing a lot of effort in creating content and keeping up with trends in the hopes of eventually landing the sponsorship you're after.

To maintain reader interest and your appeal to advertisers, you must continue posting even when you have the sponsored content you want. That entails making a larger time and financial commitment, even though you have a lot of flexibility in terms of when to do it.

Opportunity: Although driving is required, this is a terrific opportunity to make hundreds of dollars each month for little to no additional cost if you're already putting in the mileage. It is possible to pay drivers per mile.

Risk: Find a reputable organization to collaborate with if this concept piques your interest. In this area, a lot of con artists set up schemes in an attempt to defraud you of thousands.

agency will "wrap" the advertisements around your automobile for free. Newer vehicles are preferred by agencies, and drivers have to have an impeccable driving history.

Opportunity: Although driving is required, this is a terrific opportunity to make hundreds of dollars each month for little to no additional cost if you're already putting in the mileage. It is possible to pay drivers per mile.

Risk: Find a reputable organization to collaborate with if this concept piques your interest. In this area, a lot of con artists set up schemes in an attempt to defraud you of thousands.

- Invest in a savings account or certificate of deposit with a high yield.

Investing in an online bank's high-yield savings account or certificate of deposit (CD) can earn you one of the highest interest rates in the nation in addition to a passive income. Making money won't even require you to leave your home.

Opportunity: To get the most out of your CD, just look out for the best savings accounts or CD rates in the country. Because you may choose the best rate in the nation, using an Internet bank is typically far more advantageous than using a local one. Additionally, if your financial institution is FDIC-backed, you will still be eligible for a guaranteed return of principal up to a maximum of $250,000.

Risk: Your principal is secure as long as your bank is FDIC-insured and operating within reasonable bounds. Thus, the safest return on investment is typically found when making a savings account or CD purchase. However, the real purchasing power of your money may be negatively impacted by that return if inflation is taken into account. Even so, investing in a certificate of deposit (CD) or savings account will generate higher returns than keeping cash on hand or depositing money into a checking account that pays no inter est.

Part four

- Give your house a short-term rental

This simple method converts unutilized space into a source of income by making use of it. Consider renting out your present apartment while you're away if you have a summer vacation planned, must be away from home for an extended period, or are simply looking to travel.

Possibility: You can list your place and determine the terms of rental on a variety of websites, like Airbnb and Vrbo. If you rent to a tenant who may be there for a few months, you'll get paid for your work with little additional effort.

Risk: While there isn't much of a financial risk involved, having strangers stay in your home carries a danger that isn't typical of most passive investments. For instance, tenants may steal items or even damage or destroy your prop
Atty.

- Advertise on your car

You may be able to earn some extra money by simply driving your car around town. Contact a specialized advertising agency, which will evaluate your driving habits, including where you drive and how many miles. If you're a match with one of their advertisers, the agency will "wrap" your car with the ads at no cost to you. Agencies are looking for newer cars, and drivers should have a clean driving record.

Opportunity: While you do have to get out and drive, if you're already putting in the mileage anyway, then this is a great way to earn hundreds per month with little or no extra cost. Drivers can be paid by the mile.

Risk: If this idea looks interesting, be extra careful to find a legitimate operation to partner with. Many fraudsters set up scams in this space to try and bilk you out of thousands.

- Create a YouTube channel or blog.

Are you an authority on visiting Thailand? A master of the game Minecraft? A swing-dancing sultan? Use your enthusiasm for a topic to create a blog or YouTube channel, then monetize it with sponsors or adverts. Choose a well-liked topic, even a narrow specialty, and become an authority on it. As you gain recognition for your interesting content, it can eventually generate a consistent revenue stream. Initially, you'll need to develop a library of content and attract readers.

Possibility: By utilizing a free or extremely inexpensive platform, you can attract readers with your excellent material. Your chances of being recognized as "the" person to follow are higher the more distinctive your voice or area of interest. Draw sponsors to you after that.

Risk: It may take some time to develop the initial content and continue producing new material. Additionally, you'll need to have a strong sense of love for the product because this will keep you motivated to keep going, especially in the beginning when people are still finding you.

The main drawback is that if there is minimal interest in your topic or specialty, you could invest a lot of time and money with little return. You may find that your field of expertise is too specialized to attract a profitable audience, but you won't know for sure until y
ou try.

● Renting out practical household goods
This is an alternative to hiring out a vacant vehicle: Start even smaller when it comes to other home items that you may have lying around the garage that folks could use. Mowers of lawns? Strong instruments? Tools for mechanics and a toolbox? Big coolers or tents? Seek expensive goods that are only occasionally needed by consumers

and for which it might not make sense for someone to acquire. Next, arrange for a method for customers to find your merchandise and a means of making a payment for it.

Opportunity: If there's interest in a specific sector, you can scale up from a tiny starting point. As it grows warmer or colder, do people suddenly want a tent for a weekend camping trip? Instead of keeping the item on hand, you could even go buy it once you determine where the demand is. After using the item a few times, you might be able to recover its worth in certain situations.

Risk: Although property theft or damage is always possible, you can reduce this risk by drafting contracts that let you replace lost or stolen property at the client's expense. You won't be taking on much danger if you start small, especially if you currently own the item and won't likely need it very soon. Liability concerns should get extra

consideration, particularly if you are renting out potentially hazardous equipment (such as power to
ols).

- Make internet sales of designs

If you're good at designing, you could be able to generate money by selling products that have your printed designs on them. You may sell products with your designs on T-shirts, hats, mugs, and more through companies like CafePress and Zazzle.

Possibility: You can start with your creations to gauge market demand before growing from there. You might be able to take advantage of the heightened interest in a current event by creating a shirt that, at the very least, satirically depicts the spirit of the moment. To market your goods, you may also create your online storefront using a platform like Shopify.

Risk: One of the main hazards of tying up your capital is avoided when you use printing partners to transport products without having to directly invest in the goods yourself. However, if you purchase some of the merchandise yourself, you might be able to negotiate a lower price. The possibility of investing a lot of time with little return is another significant risk, but if you're already working on design projects for other reasons, like personal interest, this path can be worthwhile.

Part five

- Establish an annuity

A steady source of income can be established with an annuity. Typically, an annuity involves you giving money to a financial institution—usually an insurance company—in exchange for a future income stream. Annuities can be set up to start paying out immediately or much later. Annuities pay out every month.

Opportunity: Annuities are the epitome of passive income and may be set up in a multitude of ways, based on your specific needs. The insurance company can arrange for an instant monthly payout if that is what you desire, or you can schedule the payment to begin, say, upon your retirement. Furthermore, you have the option to set up an annuity with a fixed return or one that can pay out differently based on how well the annuity's investments performed.

A lifelong payout or a predetermined amount of time, like 20 years, might be specified for an annuity. Upon your passing, it might stop making payments, or it might keep making payments to your spouse. There are lots of alternatives.

Risk: Annuities can be very complicated and can lock you in for a long period, however, you may be able to get out by paying a large penalty. To grasp the benefits and drawbacks of the particular contract, carefully read the fine print.

Since each annuity contract is unique, it may provide a distinct combination of benefits to meet your needs. Therefore, it's critical to comprehend what you're agreeing to.

- Purchase a small company

You have the opportunity to create a steady stream of income from an established firm by starting a local business. If the company is profitable enough, you might even be able to appoint a manager to oversee it while you take on minimal or no decision-making duties. To purchase it and avoid risking too much of your own money upfront, you might be able to secure an enticing loan.

Possibility: You could be able to invest in lucrative and alluring local company niches that are difficult for rivals to enter. Especially in the beginning when you're getting up to speed, you might be able to capitalize on the seller's experience or credentials. Sellers have an incentive to see the firm prosper if they are ready to finance a portion of the transaction. Also, you may make part of the purchase price reliant on specified profit goals or other criteria.

Risk: You run the risk of purchasing a company that has fading prospects or is far less profitable than it first appears. For this reason, you should thoroughly screen any possible acquisition candidates. To secure

the greatest offer and prevent problems, it can be beneficial to work with seasoned and trustworthy brokers. You can also employ a consultant to help you assess a potential deal. Furthermore, you should ensure that the manager you choose to oversee the store is trustworthy and capable; otherwise, you may run into is
sues.

- Purchase a blog

Consider purchasing one instead of waiting in line to create one if you want to enter the blogging world. Along with maybe being able to bring your own, you can obtain the past owner's contacts and ties. And instead of creating and expecting, you can start making money right away.

Possibility: Purchasing a blog allows you to enter the market immediately rather than later, but you should already be an expert and ardent enthusiast. If you can think of a few ways to make the blog better—better content, increased efficiency, cheaper expenses, etc.—it will help you leverage it into a larger return than the purchase price may have suggested.

Risk: A blog, like any business, is not very liquid, so you might not be able to sell it for what you paid for it or at all if you decide you want to move on to something greener. Naturally, you also need to be able to accurately assess the market and create content that draws in advertisers and other revenue-generating sources as well as reades.

● Purchasing preferred stock

One kind of stock that behaves more like a bond is preferred stock, which pays out high, enticing dividends regularly. Preferred stock, like bonds, has a face value and could have a set maturity. It could alternatively be perpetual, in which case the corporation wouldn't have to redeem it. It can usually be redeemed five years after it is issued. Preferred stocks have strong liquidity and are easily obtainable because they trade on an exchange.

Possibility: Compared to bonds, preferred stock may pay out higher-than-usual dividends; but, this comes at the expense of missing out on a capital gain (unless preferreds are purchased at a discount to face value). However, it might be a tempting method to generate a passive income. Preferreds are issued by a large number of banks, REITs, and other financial institutions to fund their operations.

Risk: Because preferred stocks are traded on an exchange, there is a chance that their price will change, especially in reaction to shifts in the current interest rate environment. Preferred price will probably decrease when rates rise and vice versa, albeit it probably won't increase significantly over face value. Similar to bonds, you must thoroughly research the firm and its capacity to pay dividends; otherwise, the value of your investment may drop over time.

Choose a preferred stock fund instead of individual preferred equities if you don't want to pick them. Your risk will be lower because you'll receive a diverse assortment of preferreds.

- Invest in a closed-end fund for municipal bonds.

Municipal bonds provide investors with tax-free dividend income in return for funding state and local government projects. A closed-end fund that invests in this segment of the market owns a range of these bonds and then uses borrowing to purchase more to increase overall return. Closed-end funds are the most passive kind of income, much like CDs or dividend funds.

Possibility: Earning tax-free income through a closed-end municipal bond fund could be appealing, particularly for individuals residing in states with high tax rates or in higher tax brackets. Because these funds use leverage, which carries some risk of its own, they often offer higher dividends than ordinary municipal bonds. However, because a fund owns a variety of different bonds, total risk is reduced. Generally speaking, closed-end funds should be acquired at a substantial discount to their net asset value to lower risk.

Risk: When interest rates rise, bond prices and, consequently, the price of bond funds, decrease (and vice versa). However, the leverage of a closed-end fund amplifies this impact, meaning that in a downturn, the average fund will lose more than the average bond. To cover higher borrowing costs, the bond fund might also have to reduce its distribution, which would raise the fund's price even further. Because interest rates fluctuate quickly, a closed-end fund may be Vola
tile.

What is the best passive income source?
The greatest passive income source will rely on several criteria, the most significant of which are your financial resources, the magnitude of the opportunity overall, your aptitude and level of interest in the field, the time commitment required, and the likelihood of success. Less entry barriers are usually associated with a more crowded market of competitors and a lesser chance of success.

Therefore, you will need to compare the opportunity to these elements and determine which passive income technique is most effective for you. However, having a natural aptitude and enthusiasm for the field you want to work in might be beneficial since these will spur you on throughout the harder early going.

Both individuals who have some money to start with and those who don't have any can find prospects for passive income.

Without any money, how can I generate passive income?
You will mostly need to rely on your time commitment to get by if you start with little to no money, at least until you start to accumulate any. This entails concentrating on passive income opportunities that benefit from the following characteristics:

a field in which you excel. Here, you can develop your skills into a product or service that will benefit customers, such as software development or design.
a labor-intensive, up-front opportunity. You'll need to take advantage of an opportunity that calls for a time or labor commitment, like developing an influencer profile or making a course.
Until you can obtain enough capital to increase your pool of opportunities, you are essentially substituting your time for your lack of capital.

What is the ideal number of sources of income?

When it comes to producing income streams, there is no "one size fits all" solution. Your current financial situation and your future financial objectives should determine how many sources of income you have. But it's a good idea to start with at least a few.

"You'll catch more fish with multiple lines in the water. "A wonderful method to diversify your income stream is to include rental properties, income-producing securities, and entrepreneurial endeavors in addition to the earned income produced by your human capital.

Naturally, you want to ensure that working on a new passive income source won't take your attention away from your existing ones. Therefore, you should balance your efforts and make sure you're allocating your time to the most beneficial chances.

Reduce your income tax liability.

Although passive income is a terrific way to supplement your income, your efforts will result in a tax liability. However, by incorporating and opening a retirement account, you may lessen the tax burden and get ready for the future as well. However, not all of these passive techniques will benefit from this tactic, and to be eligible, your fi

rm must be genuine.

Register with the IRS and receive a tax identification number for your business.

Then contact a broker who can open a self-employed retirement account.

Determine which kind of retirement account might work best for your needs.

Two of the most popular options are the solo 401(k) and the SEP IRA. If you stash the cash in a traditional 401(k) or SEP IRA, you can take a tax break on this year's taxes. The solo 401(k) is great because you can stash up to 100 percent of your earnings into the account, up to the annual maximum.

Meanwhile, the SEP IRA allows you to contribute only at a 25 percent rate. In addition, the solo 401(k) permits you to make an additional contribution of up to 25 percent of your profits in the business.

If you're thinking of going this route, compare the differences between the two account types or look at the best retirement plans for the self-employed.